Everyone has to go to the dentist often in their life. We all go. But we try to look after our teeth between visits too.

Note to parents

Learning to overcome the mixed feelings of a visit to the dentist can be very difficult for children. Their feelings (both good and bad) are often the result of previous visits and the influence they receive from others, including from media such as television. It is very important to introduce children to the reasons why we have dentists, and rather than associate them with feelings of anxiety to show that they are part of the process of maintaining good dental health.

In this book we look at Joanne, her brother and a friend, as they each make routine visits to the dentist. We describe what happens and explain some of the reasons why children visit the dentist.

The author

Pamela J Coates BDS VU (MANC) LDS RCS (ENG) is a dentist who works in Manchester.

TANYA GUNNARSDOTTIR

Visit to the Dentist

written by Pamela J Coates
illustrated by Lynne Byrnes

 Published in Great Britain by
World International Publishing Ltd., an Egmont Company,
Egmont House, PO Box 111, Great Ducie Street,
Manchester M60 3BL. Printed in Germany.
ISBN 0 7498 0115 8

A CIP catalogue record for this book is available from the British Library

At home we drink lots of milk to make our teeth strong. We have lots of fresh fruit and vegetables to eat. They are better for our teeth than sticky sweets and puddings.

At school we learn that some things are bad for teeth, like rock, chewing gum, toffees and fizzy drinks.

It is better to have an apple or a packet of crisps at playtime than sweets.

We always brush our teeth after breakfast and before we go to bed.

Our toothpaste has fluoride in it. It tastes nice and minty. We don't need to use very much. A squirt about the size of a pea is the right amount.

We spend a long time cleaning our teeth. It takes at least three minutes to clean all our teeth properly.

We must be sure to brush the back of our teeth as well as the front and to clean in between our teeth too.

The postman delivered a card from our dentist. It was time we had our check-ups.

Would you like to know what our last visit to the dentist was like?

We sat in the reception room while we waited for our turn to see the dentist.

There were comics and magazines on a table for us to read while we waited and some toys for the very young children to play with.

Hello.

The nurse showed us into the surgery to meet our dentist.

The nurse checked our toothbrushing by painting our teeth with red liquid which showed the dirt left on them. She showed us how to clean our teeth properly.

My brother got a sticker to put in his book because he had brushed his teeth properly.

The dentist counted my teeth. She used a little mirror to see the back ones. She checked to make sure that none of them were going bad with decay.

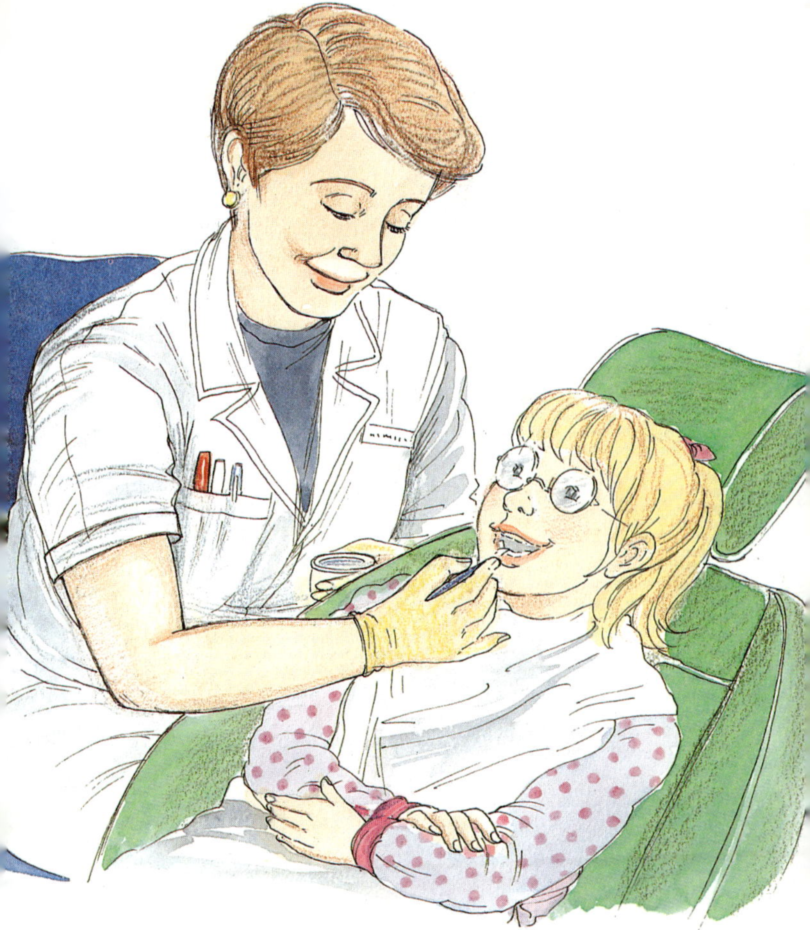

I had grown some new back teeth so the dentist put something on the top of them to help stop decay. Then the dentist polished my teeth.

My brother had been wearing a brace to straighten his teeth. The dentist had taken out two side teeth to make room for the teeth at the front.

The dentist looked to see how his teeth were moving. The wires of the brace had moved the teeth into the space and straightened them. He looked much better.

My friend needed a filling because he had some decay in a back tooth. The dentist said he had eaten lots of sweets.

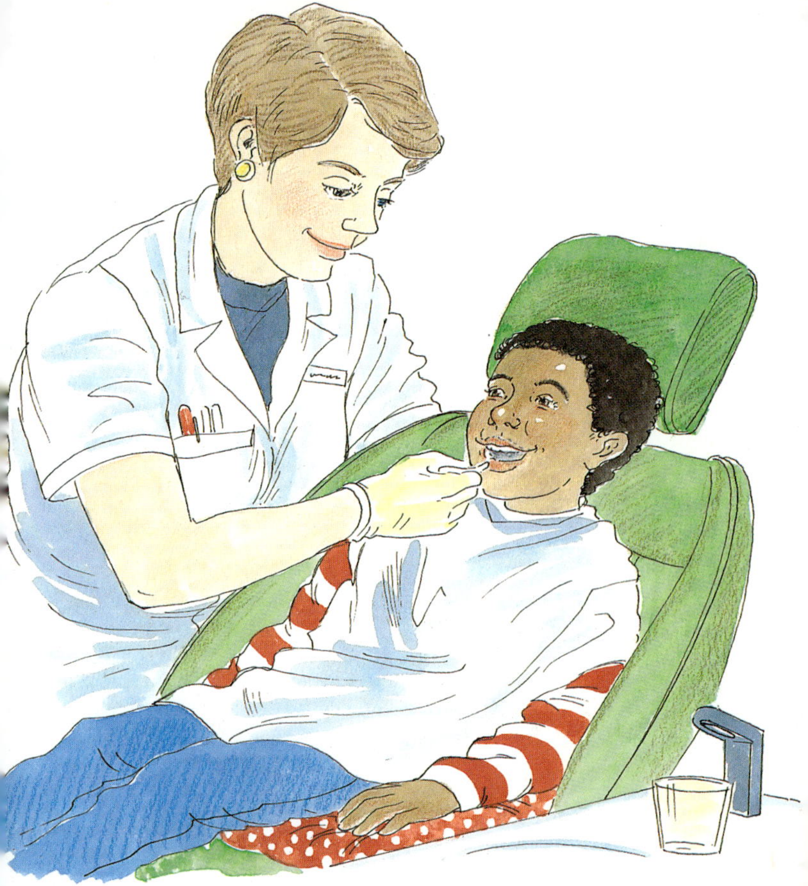

First the dentist put the tooth to sleep with special cream. Then she used a drill to clean out the decay.

The nurse mixed some filling cement for the dentist to put in the hole in the tooth.

When everything was done my friend washed his mouth out with special pink water. He chose some stickers for being good and put them in his sticker book.

When we were finished we went back to the reception room while Mummy made another appointment.